Ooh la la!

How to be Infuriatingly French

Mimi Malone

summersdale

OOH LA LA!

Summersdale Publishers Ltd
46 West Street
Chichester
West Sussex
PO19 1RP
UK

www.summersdale.com

Printed and bound by Tien Wah Press, Singapore

ISBN: 1-84024-665-0
ISBN 13: 978-1-84024-665-0

Contents

Food and drink

Being French, you'll need to be extremely fussy about your bread, so never buy a whole baguette. Instead, buy a fresh half baguette in the morning for breakfast, and then another fresh half baguette at lunchtime. Never buy bread that would actually stay fresh longer than a few hours.

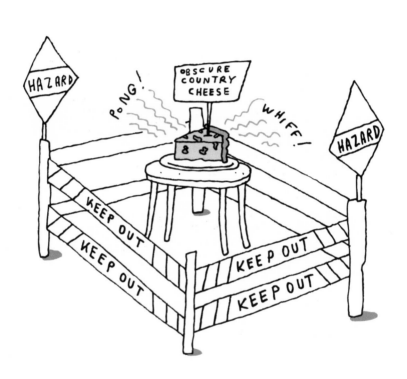

When selecting a cheese, always smell it first to find the most flavoursome. A general rule of thumb: if you can't knock someone out with your breath after eating it, and if it doesn't smell like cowpats, then it probably needs more time to mature.

If you really want to fit in, order *escargots* in garlic butter when dining out. Though you might at first find their slimy texture alarming, in time you will learn to appreciate this mollusc-based national dish. If snails are not available, get the taste buds going with a salad made with *gésiers*, or duck gizzards.

Live on a diet of *croissants au beurre,*
quiche Lorraine and *tarte au citron,* but
maintain a strict regimen of talking
non-stop about politics and waving
your arms about between meals in
order to remain svelte.

Never drink instant coffee or order a coffee to take away. Your coffee of choice should be ordered at a *café* and sipped slowly for hours as you watch the world go by – even though it's only the size of a child's toy teacup.

An evening out with friends should be spent in a civilised manner, perhaps dropping into a few *cafés* and bars and consuming a tiny round glass of *vin* or *bière*, but should never descend into drunken revelry. The only exception to this rule is the launch party for Beaujolais Nouveau in late November. On this night it is customary to drink atrociously bad red wine by the bottle, sometimes even from the bottle, spend the evening roving the streets singing raucously with friends and the next day recovering from the worst type of hangover.

Meander down to the *marché* with your *coffin* (woven basket) to buy soil-covered vegetables and mouldy cheese for that special gourmet dinner. Always ask where everything is from. The market stall owners are the keepers of all knowledge and will tell you exactly when and how their perfect produce should be eaten.

Etiquette

When waiting to board a bus, resist the urge to form an orderly queue or wait your turn. Instead, use whatever means available, including nudging, elbowing and tactical use of any piece of luggage that you might be carrying, to work your way to the front. When in a *boulangerie*, however, an older person has the right to be served ahead of a younger person, regardless of how long they've been waiting.

When meeting friends remember your kisses or *'bisous'*. The number will vary from two to four, depending on where you are and the regional background of those you are greeting: you must judge which is appropriate for each situation so as to avoid embarrassment. When greeting a group of four friends in a town where four kisses is the norm, prepare to be there a while. Don't forget the same procedure when the meeting is over.

Never enter and leave a shop without saying *'Bonjour Madame'* and *'Au revoir Madame'*. When conversing with strangers, however, don't feel obliged to offer your name, and be offended should anyone ask for it – and never ask what someone does for a living.

When planning your day, don't forget to factor in a three-hour lunch break, which should be spent enjoying a leisurely meal with the customary glass of wine and post-lunch siesta. Under no circumstances should you reduce yourself to eating at your desk or, worse still, be seen scoffing a sandwich on your way down the street.

If your ear starts itching when you're out in public, abandon discretion, clench your hand into a tight fist, extend your little finger, or *auriculaire*, insert it into your ear and give it a good old shake around in there.

If you witness a small child fall over,
or go *badaboum*, as it is said in French,

be helpful enough to point out to the
child that they have indeed fallen
over by saying 'Oh, *badaboum!*'

Wish your fellow diners *'Bon appétit!'* at the start of the meal. You may be inclined to observe wittily to your fellow Frenchmen that there is no equivalent for this in English, because English food is so bad.

Out and about

Learn to extract Formula One performance from an unroadworthy little car with a 1-litre engine.

Drive with the conviction that you have right of way in all situations, for example when overtaking on a blind turn. Hoot your horn randomly and regularly, and regard the sight of a pedestrian setting foot onto a zebra crossing as an invitation to accelerate. Always assume that you have priority over drivers already on a roundabout.

When choosing a pet, observe carefully to detect what type of dog is the fashionable choice in your town, for some regions will prefer rat-like proportions while others opt for heftier breeds. Ignore your pet's tendency to do its business on the pavement, for this is the dog's right as a citizen of France. Should it decide to relieve itself on the doorstep of a restaurant, this may be seen as a comment on the establishment.

Dress your children impeccably at all times, with colour-coordinated outfits in the latest style. They should be instructed to behave in a civilised manner from an unnaturally early age. Ensure that your children conform to accepted French modes of behaviour (such as only shoplifting and being rude when on school trips to England) and don't put up with any nonsense – sharply use the phrase '*Ça suffit!*' (that's enough) whenever they step out of line.

You're driving through town on a one-way road and you spot a friend, or need to stop to buy bread. Do you find a parking space? Of course not. Simply stop where you are and proceed, ignoring the beeping horns of the cars stuck behind you. If you have to leave the car for a longer period of time, don't be afraid to make use of the pavement or disabled parking spaces – just aim for a space that fits or might fit your car.

Language

If someone asks you a question, you are not obliged to formulate a coherent reply: you can simply respond by shrugging your shoulders, raising your eyebrows and uttering *'Bof'*.

When you hear a foreigner trying to speak French, make it clear by your tone and demeanour that you are disgusted by their futile attempts to master *la langue française*.

Finish every sentence with *'quoi'*. When asked whether you can do something (especially if you're a tradesman such as a mechanic or plumber), suck in your cheeks and let out the words *'C'est pas evident.'* This will let them know that it will be tricky, and that when you do complete it successfully they should be very grateful.

When you're posing for a photograph, don't say 'cheese'. Don't say *'fromage'* either. Although thinking about the nation's favourite food should be enough to make any Frenchman smile, they prefer instead to say *'ouistiti'*. It means marmoset.

'*Impossible n'est pas français!*' It simply isn't the French way to accept defeat in the face of adversity. However, if a French person tells a non-French person that something is impossible, then it is impossible.

If you have already said hello, good morning, etc. to someone that day, you can greet them with a *'re-bonjour'*, or simply growl *'re'* at them.

Wish people well in whatever they are doing, whether having a meal (*Bon appétit*), having a nice day (*Bonne journée*), having a good journey home (*Bonne route*), finding their way into a hotel room (*Bonne installation*), doing their laundry (*Bon lavage*), or whatever they happen to be doing at the time – and which you wish them to continue to enjoy doing (*Bonne continuation*). Nothing is too insignificant to merit a little encouragement.

Leisure

When taking your *vélo* out for a leisurely spin at the weekend, kit yourself out in a fluorescent lycra all-in-one and wraparound sunglasses. Remember: the road is there for the benefit of cyclists, not other road users, so feel free to cycle two or three abreast if you're out with friends.

Heading out with friends to watch *les Bleus* play at the Stade de France? Bring along a brass instrument to play badly in the stands and warm up for your fanfare in the *métro en route* to the *stade*. If you are feeling particularly patriotic, bring a cockerel to release onto the pitch before the match – seeing the living embodiment of the French team's emblem strutting around will raise the players' spirits, and they won't mind a bit if the bird gets in their way or pecks at their ankles.

Rollerblading is *hyper* cool and is in no way less fashionable than it was back in the nineties. If you want to impress, get down to your local town park or seafront and glide around on your blades wearing sexy lycra shorts and a clingy top. You'll look even better as the sweat patches start to show through.

Develop a strong enthusiasm for skiing, since you'll be spending one week every February engaging in the nation's favourite winter activity. If you are of the older generation, be sure to invest in an all-in-one, eighties-style ski suit, which will in no way make you look foolish or stand out from the other skiers on the piste.

Les skieurs

If you're getting on a bit, fill your hours by playing *pétanque*, or boules. If entering a competition, take this sport with the utmost seriousness and if possible develop your own quirky style of throwing or show off a nifty magnetic device for picking up the ball.

Culture

Read (but not necessarily understand) the philosophies of Derrida and Sartre.

Earn a respectable living by pretending to be in a box, or pulling an imaginary rope whilst wearing full mime regalia.

Protests are a national cultural activity to bring the community together at a certain time of year, so be ready to down tools and stage a *manif* in the centre of town. The reason for action is by-the-by: what really matters is that you demonstrate in true French style. Endeavour to cause maximum disruption to public transport systems by congregating with fellow protestors on tramways and railway lines.

In France, writers, professors and all those who practise the arts are known as *intellectuels*, so if your line of work is in one of these areas, feel free to introduce yourself casually as an intellectual. Ideally you should have some square spectacles in an outlandish colour, and wear a black turtleneck jumper.

If you're writing a book, remember to put the contents page, or *table des matières*, at the end rather than the start. That way, the reader won't waste time working out which parts of the book are most relevant/useful to them: instead they will just plunge in and read the whole thing. Then, when they're done, they can skim through the list of contents and reflect on which chapters they most enjoyed.

Commerce, rules
and bureaucracy

Pay for absolutely everything with a cheque.

Remember that the customer (and especially the foreign customer) is always wrong. Barely concealed distaste and an overt sense of superiority is the right of the business owner. Do not expect to make eye contact.

La banque

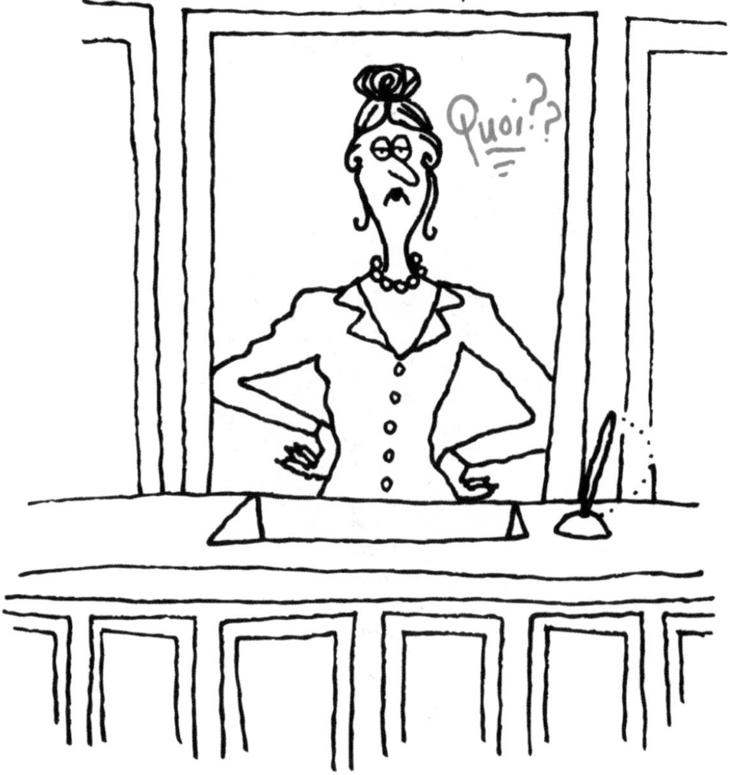

Get used to filling in forms and battling red-tape. As a citizen of France you can expect to waste many a day queueing for forms, filling them out and queueing again to hand them in. Take this as an opportunity to criticise the government loudly and scrutinise the inadequacies of French bureaucracy with your fellow queuers.

If you are employed as a civil servant, make sure you look busy and overworked at all times. If someone complains, the correct response is *'C'est normal.'* Be pedantic. If someone is required to have four photocopies of a document, it would be improper to accept three copies and make an extra at the photocopier opposite your desk. The applicant must go all the way across town to the library to make the copy and then return to join the end of the queue again.

Business and commerce are not really part of the French way of life. Do not attempt any financial transaction during the lunch hours of 12 to 3 or on a Sunday, and remember it is highly unlikely to be possible on a Monday either. And whatever you do, don't plan to effect any business or get anything at all done during the month of August, when you should join your fellow French in taking the entire month off.

No-smoking signs are not there for your attention. Feel free to ignore them and light up where and when you see fit. It is perfectly acceptable to scavenge cigarettes from fellow smokers and also understandable to display surprise if you encounter a non-smoker.

European-wide laws and regulations do not apply, of course, to the French. France is a nation of 100,000 village-based mini dictators, or 'mayors' as they are sometimes known, who actually control what you can and can't do. To get on in France you can ignore the law without fear of retribution, as long as you are in favour with the mayor. Ignore his word at your peril.

Attracting the
opposite sex

If you are a man, invest in a butch 'man-bag', usually a long-strapped purse in an appropriately masculine colour. These are perfect for carrying your *carte d'identité*, *carnet de billets* and other items that would fit just as well into your pockets.

If you are a middle-aged man, grow a moustache – the bushier the better. If you are a middle-aged woman, cut your hair short, dye it red with henna and wear really flouncy skirts.

If you are a young woman, forget about using make-up and wearing a sexy top to attract a Frenchman. The quickest way into a passionate embrace is to let him see thick clumps of black hair sprouting from your armpits. The accompanying aromas are nature's intended way for French people to attract a mate.

Believe that socialism is a good idea. As you pay so much in taxes, it is only reasonable to expect the State to do pretty much everything for you. This will make you especially attractive to students.

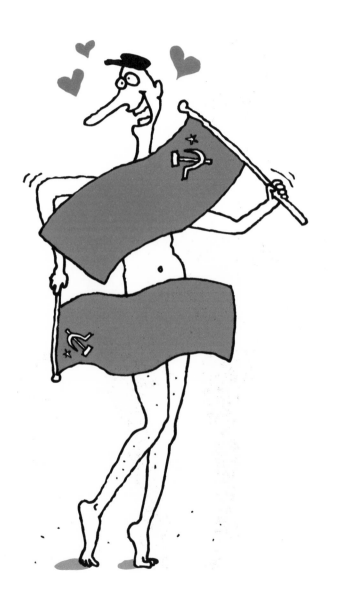

Remember: if a politician cheats on his wife, or takes part in dubious acts of a sexual nature, that's his own business. Just because he is a man of questionable personal morals this doesn't mean he is a bad politician.

www.summersdale.com